Say Ahh!
The Teeth Book

Written By Floyd Stokes
Illustrated By Mikell Worley

A Product of
SUPER READER

Dedications

MW

Sincere appreciation to all of my family
and friends who supported and encouraged me,
and to Floyd Stokes for giving
me the opportunity to illustrate my first book!

FS

To my mom, Florence
my grandmother, Ozzie Lee
great grandmother, Lou Minnie

Hey kids, get out your floss
toothpaste and toothbrush
And listen to these tips
from friends you can trust

A horse's age can
usually be determined
by its teeth.

Be sure your toothbrush is nice and soft
And after you brush make sure you floss

Beavers have long sharp upper and lower incisor teeth that they use to cut into the bark of trees, water plants and other vegetation.

Brushing your teeth
at least twice every day
will keep them clean
so they won't decay

Elephants' teeth grow from the back of the jaw and move forward as the front tooth is worn down. Each tooth drops out as it reaches the front of the elephant's jaw.

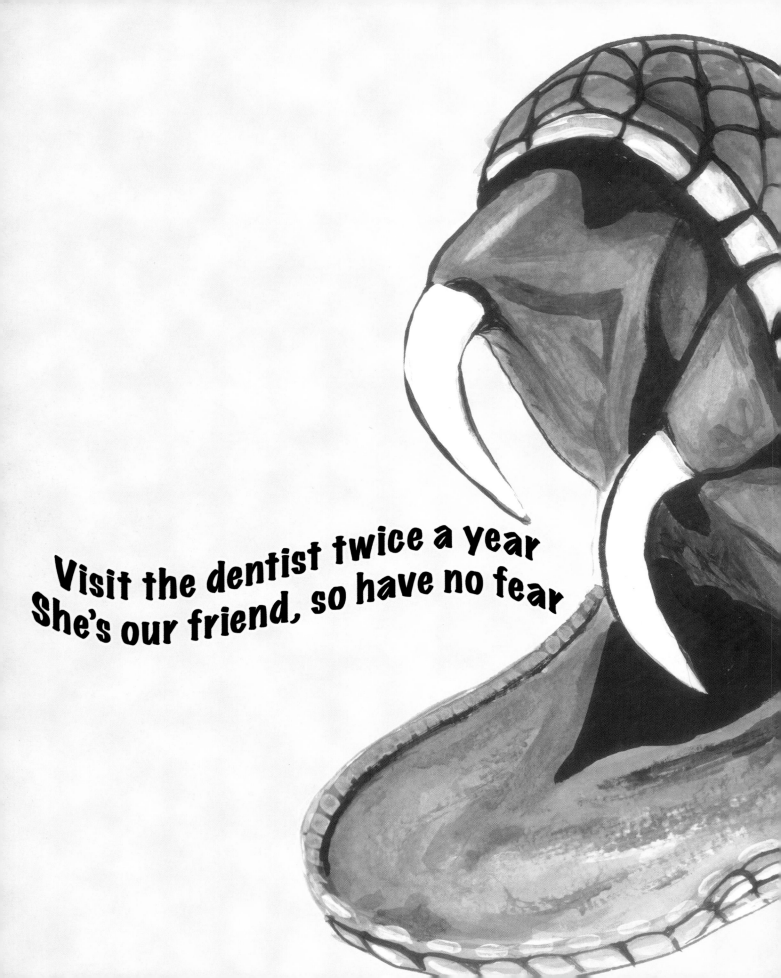

Visit the dentist twice a year
She's our friend, so have no fear

Spend two to three minutes
each time you brush
Take your time,
do your best and don't rush

A shark may have up to **30,000** teeth in its lifetime.
When one tooth is damaged or lost, it is replaced
by another. Most sharks have about **5** rows
of teeth at any time.

Eat the fruits and veggies off your plate
Drinking plenty of water is also great

Brushing after breakfast and before bedtime will keep off the dirt and the grime

Brush all your teeth
and not just the front
Change your toothbrush
every three months

All bears, whether
meat-eating or vegetarian,
have the teeth of a carnivore.
A bear's teeth grow
continuously throughout
its lifetime.

It's also important to brush your tongue
And don't forget to brush your gums

Male narwhals have the characteristic long front tooth extending approximately 8 feet and varies depending on the whale and the age.

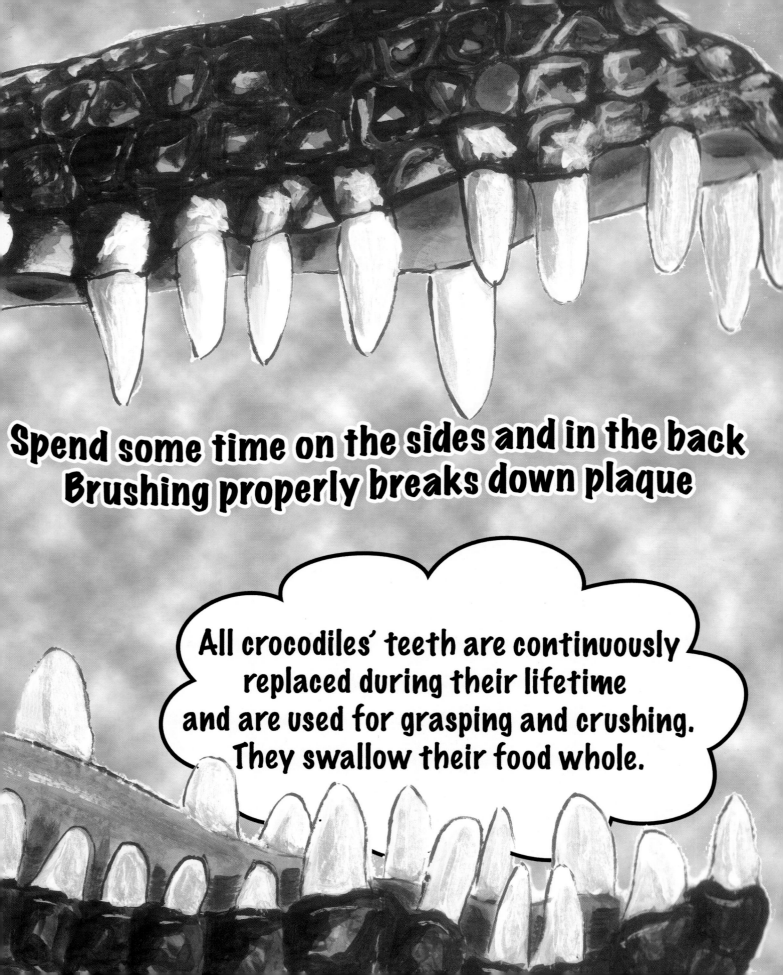

Remember, take your time
it's not a race
Brushing your teeth will
put a smile on your face

Most monkeys expose their teeth
and grimace when excited or angry.
It looks like they are smiling.

When I was in elementary school, a couple of my classmates teased me for having bucked teeth. I felt very embarrassed. As a result of being teased, I went home that day and brushed and brushed my teeth.

I decided that if I was going to be teased about having bucked teeth, then I was going to have the cleanest and whitest bucked teeth that they had ever seen. Needless to say, the teasing stopped. You too can have clean, white teeth.

Develop good habits today and they will stay with you for a lifetime.

Keep Brushing,
Floyd Stokes

Floyd Stokes is the founder and Executive Director of the American Literacy Corporation (ALC), which is a non-profit organization that promotes the importance of reading to elementary-age students up to 5th grade. SuperReader is one of the programs of the ALC. As SuperReader, Floyd Stokes has performed for over 70,000 children since 2001.

Floyd is also the author of "Teddy, The Hungry Little Bear". His high school alma mater, John F. Kennedy High School, renamed the library The Floyd "SuperReader" Stokes Library on September 2, 2007. On May 12, 2008 he received the 3rd annual James Patterson PageTurner Award.

He is married to LaShana and has five children: Dwayne, Tressimee, Devin, Madison and Olivia. He was born in Mound Bayou, Mississippi and currently lives in Harrisburg, Pennsylvania.

For more information,
please visit
www.superreader.org

Mikell Worley is delighted to have been able to combine her love of painting and nature with a project that will help children have healthier teeth! Her years of work with the State Health Improvement Plan have made her aware of the problems for children with poor oral health.

She has been an advocate for children for almost 20 years and is currently the board president of the local America's Promise (winner of the 100 Best Communities two years in a row!) and the chair of the Investing in Children and Youth Focused Care Council through the United Way of the Capital Region.

Mikell lives in a fishing cabin along the Yellow Breeches Creek in central PA where she is surrounded by inspiration for her art. She has two grown daughters and is pleased that they are carrying on her passion for weaving creativity throughout their lives.

For more information, please visit www.mikellstreasures.com

Coming winter 2008

Inspired by Floyd's four year old daughter Madison A. Stokes

Popcorn Popcorn is a book about the joy of popping and eating popcorn. It features a mother popping popcorn. The popcorn lands in the most unusual places. It then turns into some very interesting animals. Popcorn, one of America's favorite snacks, is an action packed fun filled book for children of all ages. This book is sure to get children up and moving with the animals.